AMERICA
WHY I LOVE HER

AMERICA
WHY I LOVE HER

ORIGINAL WORDS BY JOHN MITCHUM
ILLUSTRATED BY ALINA WELCH

Applewood Books
An Imprint of Arcadia Publishing
Carlisle, Massachusetts

DOES THE CALL OF THE NIAGARA THRILL YOU WHEN YOU HEAR HER WATERS ROAR?

❋ WHITE-TAILED DEER

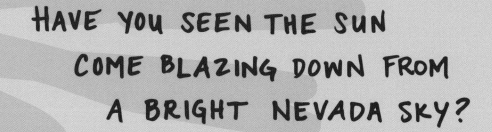

HAVE YOU SEEN THE SUN
COME BLAZING DOWN FROM
A BRIGHT NEVADA SKY?

MY HEART CRIES OUT...
MY PULSE RUNS FAST
AT THE MIGHT OF HER DOMAIN.

YOU ASK ME WHY I LOVE HER?
I'VE A MILLION REASONS WHY.
MY BEAUTIFUL AMERICA...
BENEATH GOD'S WIDE,
WIDE SKY.

Books in the "Little Duke" Series

America, Why I Love Her
978-1-4290-3030-4

The People
978-1-4290-3031-1

An American Boy Grows Up
978-1-4290-3032-8

Available from

Applewood Books

an Imprint of Arcadia Publishing

applewoodbooks.com

and other fine retailers